Praise for More Than What You See

"*More Than What You See* is the author's profoundly moving journey of self-revelation and a clarion call to his readers to embrace the present moment and LIVE!"

Reg E Walker, Spiritual Guide,
Author of *Life is Funny but It Ain't No Joke*

"In his first book, John Creveling shares his poetry and reflections of living and being in the world. His photography and visual artistry with its gorgeous explosions of colors are amazing. He's a poet who writes of his odyssey of the life he's fashioned for himself. Run, don't walk, to buy this remarkable and inspirational tour de force."

Ruth Z. Deming, Poet, Artist

"John Creveling writes about love, family, life and death with a deep sense of humility, compassion, and commitment for others. His reflections offer prophecies in the form of teachings told by a wise member of the tribe. In his book *More Than What You See*, John shares his sense of wonder and his strong connection to the 'child within' through his inspirational words, paintings and photographs. This poetic and wonderful book is a gem – a must-read for seekers and lovers. I'm already looking forward to his next book!"

Deborah Wasserman, Artist,
Museum Professional and Educator

"Truly wonderful. Each poem can stand alone, but taken together the book is far more than the sum of its parts. It belongs on the shelf of any person, care-partner, and healthcare provider dealing with Parkinson disease."

Sneha Mantri, MD, MS, University of Pennsylvania,
VA Fellow, Movement Disorders

"Conveying a deep and abiding appreciation of the gift of life, John's book of poetry, art and photographs, stirs the soul. His insights and wisdom about living life to the fullest and roaring with laughter, in spite of the physical and emotional hardships we encounter, is truly inspirational. His powerful message of dealing with adversity using the mantra *carpe diem* – 'seize this day in every way' is a wonderful blueprint on how to live a life of meaning and joy irrespective of the hand we are dealt. This book will move you to tears but will also help you celebrate your life and be grateful for all the gifts you have."

Barbara G. Shaiman, Author,
Founder/Principal, *Embrace Your Legacy*

"*More Than What You See* takes you on a powerful journey that is insightful, and humorous, yet brutally honest. Learn what it means to be 'fully alive' and be inspired for the challenges in your own life's journey."

Betty Shapiro, Artist

"John's book *More Than What You See* evoked many memories and triggered countless reactions to my own life. It touched me on so many levels and caught me by surprise with my own emotional responses to many of his reflections. John's candor and insights gave me a better appreciation and awareness of how much more I can control in my own life, each and every day!"

Steve Rukavina

"*More Than What You See* is a splendid collection of poetry and personal reflections from someone who is experiencing the full scope of life as few others have. John's writing is thoughtful, spiritual and will stir your emotions. A meaningful and worthwhile read!"

Walter R. Bateman

"An extraordinary book that everyone can relate to. It gave me the motivation and passion to live even those 'ordinary' days completely and with gratitude! A poetic biography, beautifully expressed with honesty, humor, and most of all, love! I want to read it again and again!"

Diane Rukavina

"John has created a book whose every word is to be savored and treasured. His wisdom and insights will surely resonate with and inspire all sentient beings."

Steven Rudner, DMD, RD

"I swam in the ebbs and flows of reading *More Than What You See*. John's deeply held values, love of family and his insatiable love for Chris, his wife, is obvious. It is a love story and so much more. I enjoyed reading his night-time meditations, past themes, especially his reflections about family members. John, is an amazingly loving and gifted man – give yourself time for his words to flow through every corpuscle of your being. I see his strength, like a great tree of courage, and his wanting to grab all of life in his creative embrace. Thank you, John, for inviting me into your living and your heroic pantheon. This is a must-read book. It is love personified."

Tom Platt

MORE THAN

WHAT YOU SEE

Poetry, Art, and Photography *03/03/19*

Anne & Allan,

Wishing you more days of awe and wonder and an abundance of ways! (page 165)

J P Creveling

JOHN P. CREVELING

v

Library of Congress Cataloging-in-Publication Data in process.
ISBN 978-1-54393-665-0

Dedication

Christina H. Robertson, my beloved wife. Your unwavering love, unbridled enthusiasm, and encouragement have emboldened me to go farther than I ever imagined possible. You are my best friend, and this book is here because of you. Thanks also for reminding me when I need it not to take myself too seriously, and to laugh often! *I love you.*

To Our Families, Lars, John Jr., Erik, Susanne, Amanda, Nate, Tido, Christopher, and John. Kat, Bradley, Amber, Macy, Sean, John III, Lauren, Ryan, Will, Charlie, Mae, Hattie, Lulu, and Eden. *Carpe diem*!

To those with health challenges who have the strength to decide their illness or condition does not define them.

Thanks to all of you who raise funds and participate in research. Your efforts help to make life better for those with Parkinson's disease and contribute to conquering the disease.

Michael J. Fox, who has dedicated himself to eradicating Parkinson's disease, you shine light and make us all proud.

Also, the late courageous Muhammad Ali. WOW!

Contents

More Than What You See

Foreword

"Most days I wake up in the morning with excitement and enthusiasm. Regardless of the weather. I determine how I will embrace the day. Not the randomness of the weather, which I have no control over," John Creveling tells me. With a twinkle in his eye and a zest for living, he acknowledges how he begins his day with a simple refrain, one that reflects his beliefs, that "every day is a beautiful day." He's also about to write another one of his eloquent reflections on the life he savors moment-by-moment and lives "the best I can while I can." He lives now with Parkinson's disease (PD) which he adamantly refuses to allow diminish his joy of being.

John says he could focus on the negative side of this "for now" incurable disease but believes life is too important to spend worrying about an unknowable future. "That is not to say I'm not concerned, that there is not some sadness associated with having PD," admits John, who is not a man in denial.

"I don't always want to talk about PD. After all, I'm so much more than my PD. We're all going to die one day. That's an irreversible fact. I want to focus on living life fully, now. I want to laugh, and I do mean laugh. How sad the world would be without laughter." John shares his life and laughter with his wife, the lovely, ebullient Christina Robertson, who is up for any adventure that strikes them. Both previously married, spend a lot of time helping others, something John says he has wanted to do for a long time.

John, the youngest of five children, joined the military at 17 and served for a while in the infantry in Germany. This had been a childhood ambition. As an eight-year-old, he says, he wore an Eisenhower jacket and leather army chaps and dreamed of being in the military. One of his role models was Audie Murphy, a World War II hero. "The army matured me right away," John says, unarguably. "You can't be a kid anymore. You hold a rifle, and you realize that this is a weapon used for only one thing. It sobers you up pretty quickly."

Almost two years after his enlistment, he married his first wife who was from Denmark. "I learned that my dreams as a child were incompatible with married life and what I wanted for my family." After more than five years in the military, he and his wife and then two children settled in the Lehigh Valley in Pennsylvania. Shortly after that, they had two more children.

In those years, he served on the Allentown (PA) City Council, worked, among other jobs, in positions in marketing and management at a major insurance company. John worked full-time and went to college at night on the GI Bill. He received his bachelor's degree from DeSales University and ultimately earned a master's degree majoring in organizational development at Temple University in Philadelphia with a GPA of 3.90.

John and Chris began dating in 1989 and married in 1991. John recalls a specific moment when he realized he was truly in love with Chris one day when they were camping in the Catskills and stopped on the road to watch the sunset. "It was just breathtaking," he remembers. "There was poignancy in that moment as we looked at each other, there was a sparkle, one that I didn't want to end."

An accomplished photographer, John's favorite subject ever since has been sunsets (and sunrises, too!). As a couple, John and Chris have seized life—family, friends, music, movies, art, and adventures. One cold winter for a fundraiser, they plunged in and (quickly) out of the freezing Schuylkill River alongside a number of other hardy volunteers.

They both love to travel, and their first priority arriving in a foreign land is getting to know people who live there. They have a charming way of relating to others wherever they are.

John remembers a two-year-old girl in Peru whom he noticed drinking water from a plastic bottle. When the child finished, the bottle became her toy. She put it on the ground and, gleefully laughing, she kicked it over to John, who gently kicked it back. Later that day, the village honored their guests in a dance, and the little girl asked John to dance with her. It would become one of many memorable experiences in their travels together.

"I feel tremendously blessed to have lived the life I have, and continue to live. I'm married to this incredible person, who to this day, reverses my blood stream," he says with sincerity. That's John. He reminds all of us to live in the present, the here and now. "*Carpe diem*," he says robustly.

John and Chris, family and friends, have actively participated in PD research and in fundraising events to sustain studies needed for seeking a cure for PD. "I do believe a cure is possible. I still have hope it will happen in my lifetime," he tells me with optimism. This book is a treasure, written by a man who receives his pleasures from what he experiences each moment.

Judy Flander, Friend and Editor

Foreword

The title of my husband's book, *More Than What You See*, is an excellent description of who he is. While we have been married for over 25 years, I am still learning new things about him as he lives life to the fullest.

I have always known John was creative, starting with the beautiful photographs he takes, but it was not until he had more free time that I discovered he could write beautiful poetry, draw, paint, and more recently, learn to play the guitar.

Perhaps the greatest indicator of fortitude and courage is how a person faces news of loss or disease. In March of 2009, John was diagnosed with Parkinson's disease (PD), a progressive neurological disorder. Presently, there is no cure. A dear friend, who faced his own health challenges, gave us excellent advice at the time: "Learn all you can medically. Live well and surround yourself with joy and love every day."

From the moment John learned he was one of the over one-million people in the United States (seven to ten million people worldwide) who have PD, he has been proactively managing his disease through information, exercise, diet, and positive thinking. In July of 2015, he had deep brain stimulation (DBS) surgery which reduced his tremors and the medication he needs to take.

John has participated in research since 2009 and is active in the Parkinson's community.

Even though Parkinson's is a disease we both wish John did not have, we have met wonderful and creative people through the disease. Some medical researchers speculate that Carbidopa-Levodopa, a drug used to manage symptoms of Parkinson's, may stimulate creative areas of the brain and serve as a "creativity pill." I believe creativity helps us manage physical challenges and become absorbed in activities that bring us joy.

Creativity has helped John to live a life of meaning and joy despite PD. There are times he becomes so absorbed in what he is creating that he loses track of time and forgets he has the "dis-ease," perhaps because creativity enables us to actively focus on the present and contribute to the future. Returning to his creative passions motivates John to forge ahead when he is experiencing an "off" day. John's creativity has been a joy to watch unfold.

John has always valued personal growth, adventure, travel and the "joy of now." PD has encouraged us to concentrate on the present and to appreciate all we have in our lives. When one has a progressive disease, the future is uncertain and the present is the only thing we have for sure. This could be said for us all! While we may not have a physical or health challenge, our time on earth is limited. None of us knows what the future holds.

John reminds us to savor every moment of every day. It is not surprising that John's motto has always been *carpe diem*, a Latin phrase which encourages us to enjoy the pleasures of the moment without being overly concerned about the future. Translated, it means "seize the day." John is a spectacular example of this—I know of no one who does this as well.

John is my soulmate, lover, and best friend. He has helped me live life more fully. On the pages that follow, John shares some treasures he has "plucked" from his daily life in the hope that it will encourage you to focus on the joyful aspects of your own. *Carpe diem*!

Christina Robertson, PhD
Author of ***Creativity and Aging:***
A Grounded Theory Study of Creative Older Adults

Prologue

Over many years, I've been writing poetry reflecting my meditations on the brevity and fragility of life. The urgent need to live in the moment, the joy of family and friends, and the memories of my own parents.

At a very early age I discovered that I loved photography and was known to carry a camera with me practically everywhere. In more recent years I found that creating art was also among my deep interests. Often, my photographs and much of my art capture cultures as well as edifices from trips with my wife, Christina Robertson.

Originally, I thought of this growing collection of my written word, photography and art as a gift, an heirloom for my children and grandchildren. The idea for turning my work into a book, *More Than What You See*, was spurred by Chris and several friends with whom I shared some of my poems, photography, and artwork.

It was not long before I had a more impelling reason for creating *More Than What You See*. In 2008, as I was beginning to think of my life, my writing, and my photography in terms of posterity, I began experiencing discomfort and numbness in my fingers, arms, and feet.

With Chris' prodding I sought medical attention. There followed X-rays, MRIs and consultations with many doctors and movement disorder specialists. On March 31, 2009 (the day before April Fools' Day!), I was diagnosed with Parkinson's disease.

Obviously, I'd heard of PD. I was aware that both the actor Michael J. Fox and the boxer Muhammad Ali had been diagnosed with the disease.

How did I first take this news? I laughed, not a typical reaction I am sure. I laughed because I was thinking about how I had dreamed of riding my motorcycle well into my senior years. (As it turned out, I continued to ride for several more years after my diagnosis.)

Of course, I never thought having PD was amusing. A few weeks after my diagnosis, one evening when Chris and I were in bed together holding each other tightly with my head on her chest, I started crying. I began to wonder how my life, our lives, would be impacted by PD. What were the implications for my children and grandchildren?

Nobody really knows the answers to those questions. My wife puts it this way, "Just as no snowflakes are alike, no one with PD responds the same." We are all unique and will uniquely experience PD. One of my most joyous snowflakes has been the discovery of enhanced creativity, most notably in my later expression through drawings and paintings, some of which you'll find on the pages of *More Than What You See*.

As I write this, there is no cure for this chronic and degenerate disease. It isn't getting any better. The number of people that will be told they have PD is estimated to be more than seven million people worldwide. Each year in the United States, between 50,000 and 60,000 people will be told they have PD. I've had a lot of time to think about it. My conclusion is simple: PD does not define me! It is not who I am as a person. As Michael J. Fox puts it, "I didn't choose to have PD, but I choose how I respond to it!"

I plan on being engaged in intentional living as best as I can for as long as I can. I fervently hope that you think of doing the same whether or not you have an illness. No one knows the hour or the day when we will depart this world. No one. Regardless of your age I urge you to get busy living! Do not waste time doing things you have no interest in. If you are uncertain what resonates with you, what sets your soul to take flight, discover ways to find your bliss.

I wish for you what I wish for myself — a life of great joy and fulfillment.

John P. Creveling
April 27, 2018

I. Living in the Moment

Valley of the Kings, Egypt

The Now That Is Today!

I speak of life,

because I can—the present,

the now that is my today.

Not of my yesterdays or my tomorrows,

they need not concern me and take away my today.

It is this day, this moment, the day that is here,

the now that is my today

I embrace completely

with all my might.

While I am able,

let me live, now.

Today.

Be Present to This Day — Today

I pray this day, today,

not be just another day

soon forgotten and among my many yesterdays.

May it be that I am fully present,

aware of this day, today.

Today I Heard a Bird Sing*

Today, I heard a bird sing
from where I did not know
but, nonetheless, I heard it sing.
Today, I saw a leaf fall from a tree.
Having reached full maturity,
it was floating to the ground, almost reluctantly,
disconnecting from its past to the present.
Today, I gazed up into the sky
as if for the very first time to see
white-cotton-like clouds
which I imagined I could walk upon
as I might please,
casting shadows onto the earth
for all those who chose to see.
Today, I caught a glimpse of innocence
when a child ran to catch a wayward butterfly,
her mother watching not far away
with an irrepressible smile on her face,
perhaps remembering when she, too,
once ran to catch a butterfly.
Today, with the one I love by my side,
I saw the sunrise over the ocean,
taking in its magical sparkle upon the water.
Holding hands, we did not need to say
what we knew to be our today.

3

John P. Creveling

Today, not some distant tomorrow,

I took a deep breath, and paused,

truly thankful for this precious gift.

* Written less than six months after my PD diagnosis in 2009

Sunshine

I saw the sun today.

It wasn't from the east,

nor was it from the west.

It was radiant,

gold, and vivid orange.

I was humbled by its beauty.

I paused

to feel its warmth

and for a moment

I was breathless.

Although occasional clouds

and rain

may impede my view,

I've learned that sometimes, too,

I may need to adjust my sight

beyond the mountains,

and tall buildings

casting shadows over the landscape.

If I look beyond the turmoil,

I know the sun is really not that far away.

It is there.

It's simply up to me to find it.

I carry a vision of the sun with me every day,

and I know its beauty

is not for me alone.

It's when I share it with others

that it gets brighter and brighter.

I hope you already know

the sun's beauty and warmth.

If not,

I'd like to share mine with you,

I carry it with me every day.

It's really not that far away.

Indiana Dunes State Park

The Gift of Rain

I love the sound of rain,

especially on a tin roof.

It takes me back to my youth.

Special places and spaces where we lived our days

with little thought of our tomorrows.

I'd like to stay there a bit longer,

if only for a short while.

Be that little boy again,

with eyes wide open,

eager to embrace each new day.

It was a time when we dreamt of finding

the pot of gold at the end of the rainbow.

Surely there would be enough money for us all.

We climbed hills and mountains effortlessly.

To the very top of the world we aspired to go.

Mt. Everest would hardly be a challenge

for us intrepid few.

Magical moments were all around us.

We found beauty in the sun rising over the ocean,

and the sun setting atop the mountains.

We boldly ventured forward as explorers,

discovering new territories and lost treasures,

although our expeditions really weren't that far from home.

Often our exploits yielded a cornucopia of gifts,

or as we called them "our bounty of treasures."

The discarded old bottle cap,

with its barely legible lettering,

appeared to be of another language.

Holding it in our hands,

we wondered how it had gotten there

and if the original container was nearby,

would it reveal its identity?

Coins, however few,

were thoroughly scrutinized.

"Who do you think held these before?

How did they get here?

Would a nickel be enough for a candy bar?"

The small piece of broken glass,

held us spellbound.

As we lifted it up to the sunlight,

it was like a kaleidoscope.

We discovered its innate beauty

that would have gone unnoticed

had we not picked it up.

We saw lightning as exhibitions

orchestrated just for us.

When we heard thunder,

we exclaimed, "The Gods are bowling."

Which ones we did not know,

or who ultimately won didn't seem to matter.

Until the games subsided,

we sought refuge in all the wrong places,

yet survived to do it again another day.

We embraced objects and experiences

that held little or no monetary value.

It was our imagination

that made us the richest of all.

I wish it would rain.

Chris in Alaska

Oh, the Joy of Being in the Forest!

I love to be in the forest amid the trees

to hear the breeze

as it shakes the leaves

like wind chimes.

They play music,

the leaves on the trees,

even those that have fallen.

I know, because I was present today

and I heard them.

They played for the animals of the forest too.

The ones I could see and the ones I could not.

We were given this gift of today.

To be present to what was then,

and what is now.

An auditory feast stimulated our senses

and played an astonishing array of masterful sounds

in celebration of our being there today.

The symphonic vibrations of music played

as if directed by the maestro himself

because we had arrived today

and not waited for another day.

Harmonies that were near,

and those distant could all be heard.

Oh, the joy of being alive and in the forest!

Dreams and Aspirations

I've always been

full of dreams and aspirations,

viewing the world

with awe and wonder.

Continuously seeking to discover

a new path,

a new way,

a new adventure.

Although I don't know how I came to believe,

I'm simply accepting.

I've always seen the glass as more than half full.

Perhaps a certain innocence has brought me here?

If so, I hope it remains with me for all of eternity.

Me, age 11

John P. Creveling

Speak to the Child Within

I sit here now with a smile on my face,
remembering when I was once young,
full of energy, innocence,
and a sense of adventure.
I recall, too,
the very first time I played
and danced in the rain.
The new blue jeans I wore
would need cleaning
and a loving mother who remembered
when she, too, was once curious.
There have been moments in my life
I remember more than others,
especially those instances when
I had no defenses nor inhibitions
that prevented me from immersing myself
into being fully alive.
I laughed without reserve
when I was unaware
and unafraid of my tomorrows.
Looking back
I realize how fortunate I was
to have lived those days.
How thankful I am to have had
a mother who encouraged my spirit,

rather than attempting to repress

the boy in me.

Perhaps now and then

I need to revisit that child within,

the one who played and danced in the rain,

keeping in my heart and mind

all that was good about those days.

The fun, the laughter,

the adventure, the journey,

and the joy of living in the world

without knowing the destination.

Mom and me, age 17, home on
leave after six months

Golden Moment

There was that moment,

well past night,

when things were stirring

within and around me,

between grogginess

and the beginning of enlightenment.

I'd like to have stayed longer,

to have lingered there for awhile

before moving on.

There was no reason to rush.

However brief it really was,

I wasn't present,

neither was I with my past.

It was a moment of innocence.

I didn't realize what was,

or what wasn't.

I woke up.

I wish I could have stayed a while longer.

Carpe Diem

I need not walk to the cliff's edge

to realize my courage,

to know I'm alive.

I've lived a storied life, it's true.

Not of mythical proportions,

no King Arthur am I.

Yet, I've gone farther

and achieved more

than I ever thought possible.

Throughout my journey

I've known some very special people

who cared enough

and shared of themselves,

who were along for more than just a ride.

They, too, were part of the experience.

Devils Tower, Wyoming

15

I'm of the age now

where I need not conceal,

or hide inside myself

that which provides and sustains me

with love and joy.

I smell a single red rose,

and in that brief moment

as I breathe in its fragrance,

I'm reminded of love,

of being loved

and giving love.

I've been brought to tears

just to see and hold

a newborn baby in my arms.

Smelled its freshness

and listened to its heart beating,

taking in and letting out

the air we take for granted.

It humbled me.

My mantra throughout my life

has been, and continues to be,

seize this day in every way.

Not to follow another's path,

but seek the one

that is meaningful to me,

the one that is my very own,

there can be no other.

I've felt the wind in my face

at an accelerated pace, yet,

I was not in a race,

except the one from within,

and that's the one

that really matters to me.

I've survived storms

that were dreary

and left plenty of people

exhausted and weary,

and some even teary.

My life has been blessed

in every way and continues to be.

There is no doubt for me

how fortunate

I am to be able to say that!

My father and me, about 14 months old.

Let It Be Said

I miss my mother and father
and many others as well.
For those who have departed
throughout the years,
I've shed my share of tears,
wishing they were still here.
I'd like to be with each of them,
to have a little more time.
Not to speak of the meaning of life,
but just to be in their presence,
perhaps feel their essence,
if only for a little while longer.
Sometimes I wish it weren't so,
but we know
which way the river flows
we are all bound to go.
The hourglass
with the sand of time,
still it flows
and won't be postponed.
The bell, too, will chime
of that there is no doubt.
The candle with its flame once so bright
flickers and catches our sight
for a brief duration

to the end of its now dimmed light.

Occasionally, I wonder,

how long it is we will live,

breathe and be?

If God will ever reveal

a golden book with a specific date

for our fate.

Although somewhere it may be written,

I doubt we will ever know.

So it is to you I appeal,

while here be present

to each and every day.

Proclaim the person you are,

live your days fully,

sometimes even boldly,

with all your strength and might,

before it is your goodnight.

Celebrate Your Life

Celebrate life
as often as you want.
You are already a winner!
Revel in being alive and aware
of the present that you have.
No one else
need determine your joy
of the days you are living.
Run, or walk up the steps.
Raise your arms in jubilation.
Drink champagne,
or no champagne at all.
Have a cake with candles on it,
or a cake without candles.
You decide
what is to be your delight.
But, I say to you celebrate—
celebrate this life you are living!

Paris, France

21

Ode to Frivolity

It is silliness and frivolity
I encourage all to know intimately.
There will be those who will readily accept this challenge
and those who will not.
Some, too, will hesitate,
as they've had little experience
with mirthful laughter.
Those who are more proficient
and have known unabated hilarity
should feel free to share
their talents and abilities
with the unskilled.
May we also know civility
and humility
as we evoke laughter for all ages,
creeds, classes, and races.
All peoples are encouraged to particpate.
No one will be denied.
Undiminished robust laughter
may at times
make some people red in the face.
But that's alright,
as long as it is never our intention to disgrace,
demean, or make anyone feel out of place.

May you roar with laughter

more often than not,

for there is no reason

or need to hold back.

Let's encourage each other

to laugh more frequently,

so much that we forget

where we are and we might feel

as if we were in outer space,

at least on another planet

because we are laughing so much!

Chris in Morocco

Table Mountain,
Cape Town, South Africa

II. Living with Challenges

Mirror art with me in the middle

Wanted Man

Unexpectedly
I caught a glimpse of you today
while I skipped a beat
walking down the street.
I struggled with memories
of days before I knew you.
Sometimes I catch myself thinking
I wonder how you found me.
I did not seek you out.
I got out of bed one day
and there you were.
I didn't invite you in
but you had settled within.
The world is round
yet here I am bound
and constrained.
At times I feel like a prisoner.
A wanted man
with a number on my back
visible for all to see,
there will be no hiding from you.
Wishing it were different
will not change a thing I know.
Better to focus on the reality
of living fully while I can.

I don't want to be reminded

of how it used to be.

For all of us, an end will come,

like a period at the end of a sentence.

How we arrive there

is the real story.

It's when I see you I realize

I want to be on another path

and still another journey.

Yet, here we are together,

an odd couple,

where you won't relinquish

your hold over me.

There is no hiding from you.

Wherever I go,

you're there with me

and always will be.

Although I still struggle with that.

I thought of you today

not because I wanted to.

Dedicated to all those people
who have a medical challenge.

Dark Horse

Like a dark horse

not expected to be in the running,

I've come from behind.

I wasn't the one others thought

to be here at this place,

this moment in time.

The miles I've traveled

and detours encountered

slowed me down now and then,

there's no denying that.

There were times, too,

when I wasted energy

on things that really

shouldn't have mattered at all.

Along the way

I discovered myself, me.

And that has made the difference,

between slowing down

and moving forward—at a pace that matters to me.

No More Tears Shed

You taunt me and tease me,

and at times I may hesitate.

For a brief moment,

I forget who you are.

Yet, we both know

you're really not far away.

You have your talons firmly in me,

and I'm sure you have no desire to leave me.

Sometimes you are present with a vengeance,

as if you want to show your omnipotence over me.

You need not demonstrate

or continue to wreak havoc in my life.

I know who you are,

you've been around a long time.

All these years later,

I'm still not ready to surrender.

I continue to be a dreamer.

There are things I yet want to do,

and places I wish to see.

I want to share memories with people, too,

and love them a while longer.

I dream someday I'll look over my shoulder

and find you gone.

A thief no more.

During the night you were found out.

All will know who you are,

your origin revealed.

No more tears shed,

broken hearts,

dreams delayed,

sorrows sown,

or lives taken.

You will be gone from this earth,

vanquished, forever.

You Are Not Licked

So your butt has been kicked,

you may feel more than a little pricked,

and even ticked,

perhaps, too, conflicted.

But I remind you,

you are not licked.

Take It On!

This journey I'm on,

the one I didn't choose,

has had its challenges for certain.

I wish I could say

I was able to do it on my own,

I really wish I could.

No one else need follow.

I've walked farther than I imagined.

Although sometimes I've struggled,

I know in this journey

there have been thousands before me,

and millions now around the globe

on a similar journey.

A path we'd all rather not travel.

Its destination

is not one where masses

are waiting and cheering you on at the finish line.

The past two hundred years

has taken its toll.

Countless numbers in the world

have known you.

Although I may ask why,

and not fully comprehend,

it is time,

it is time we find a cure

to the maladies we've known,

Parkinson's disease being just one of many.

Wishing won't do it,

nor will ignoring the symptoms.

It is real, and it has disrupted

the lives of many

and not just those with the disease.

We must continue to be valiant and vigilant,

and take on this fight,

and it is a fight,

nothing less.

As you are able,

money is important because it funds the research needed.

But it's "we the people,"

who will win in the end.

So I ask you to

take it on,

take it on now as you are able.

Thailand

Like a Thief in the Night

It appeared stealthily,
like a thief in the night.
I don't know the moment,
day, or year.
I've tried to review my life
as if I were in a movie,
screening it in slow motion.
Still, I'm unable to pinpoint
the time I realized
something was different.
I woke up one morning
and knew something had changed.
Something was not right.
Something had been taken from me.
I don't know why it chose me.
But it did.
It came like a thief in the night.
It was unsettling at first,
especially since
it took me a while to notice
and realize what it was
that had a hold over me.
Over the years
there have been many who've tried
to find the source of Parkinson's disease.

Its causes,

the reason it is so prevalent,

how to prevent it,

and how to cure it.

Some believed Parkinson's was predetermined.

Been there a long time.

Set in motion

before a person was born,

in their DNA.

Others thought

it could have been

one's occupation or environment.

As of now,

no one knows for sure.

But the fire to learn

and conquer the disease

began more 200 years ago.

Dr. James Parkinson set out to understand

why some people were afflicted

with what he called "tumultuous motion."

His 1817 paper, "An Essay on the Shaking Palsy,"

was the first to describe symptoms of the disease

that now bears his name.

There are now several million people worldwide

who share my symptoms.

The numbers are rapidly growing.

To this day, there are no answers.

No prevention.

No cure.

Only management of symptoms

to help minimize our plight.

How far must we travel,

and how many more will be taken,

by a thief in the night?

I don't know if it's too late for me.

I'm an eternal optimist.

I want to believe we'll find a cure in my lifetime.

Certainly, my hope, my dream for you

is that you'll never know,

you'll never hear

of a loved one

having Parkinson's disease.

Let it end.

Let it end with me.

Fripp Island, South Carolina

This Day, Today, I Wanted to Be Different

I rose, this day a little slower than I usually do.

Last night as I closed my eyes there was that moment

between being awake and my dreams.

I remember,

I remember wanting this day to be different,

different than my yesterdays.

Different,

not in ways that remove me from the world,

but in ways that keep me connected

to the now, that is, the present.

My yesterdays were not of sorrow, nor of regret.

But of living.

Of loving,

of being loved.

Of life.

Of fully living in the world.

Aware.

Aware.

Aware. Still,

I wanted this day to be different.

For those that came before me,

and those still following.

I wanted this day, today,

to be different.

Free.

Free to awake not with barriers,

bound from within.

But liberated.

No more living in the shadows.

I wanted this day,

this day, today, to be different,

for more than myself.

For loved ones,

loved ones all.

Woman and child in Antigua, Guatemala

Words That Empower

I emphatically acknowledge

here and now

my profound dislike

for the words *can't* and *ain't.*

I know you'll not faint

as I state

I am myself no saint.

I readily admit that my lexicon,

although not replete,

on occasion has included these words

and others I now disdain and paint

as horrid and quaint.

This is my complaint.

They restrict and may lead to personal constraint

and individual portraits that may taint

themselves as negative and unable,

even incapable.

I'd rather we acquaint

ourselves with words

that empower and embolden us

to go forward.

In seeking to attain new heights,

we discover there is no kryptonite

that will limit our flight.

We are alright and even very bright!

Haunted Memories

There are times when
I wish it were as simple as
pressing a delete button,
erasing haunting memories
of unsettled days gone by.
What is it about the past
that grips us like a vice?
We're unable to extricate ourselves
from what holds us back
and keeps us on the same path.
We struggle to distinguish
between good and bad,
right and wrong,
what we did,
or what we didn't do.
So we continue to repeat,
and wonder,
what will it take to discard
and forget those haunting memories?

Life's Journey
with an Unscheduled Detour

Most days I'm accepting of this path

arbitrarily chosen for me,

without my consent.

This is a journey no one plans for - ever.

It's a detour from what I had hoped,

what I wanted this time in my life to be about.

Yet, I will not yield,

I will not allow it to take from me

my voracious appetite for living

and celebrating the beauty that surrounds me

in nature and people.

I will be present to this day,

this moment, and

to the now that is.

I refuse to permit it to enter

my sacred space

where I keep my innocence,

the child in me,

my voice, and

my dreams.

I still dream you know.

This uninvited guest to which I am host

has taught me new lessons,

ways of living,

of interacting in the world

although I would have preferred

not to have learned them at all.

There are days I want to rail,

to rave.

I want to scream.

I want to climb the distant mountain

to its very peak,

shouting out for all those who will listen:

I will not "go gentle into that good night."*

* From the poem *Do Not Go Gentle into That Good Night*, by
Dylan Thomas

Guatemala

Just Me — Wanting to be Normal

I want to be normal.

I want to be me,

the real me.

Not the person who has emerged

in a body far detached and

unrecognizable from the person I've been

for more than 50 years —

how liberating it is to say that.

I want to be "*normal*" again.

Whatever normal means.

Not the kind of normal that I'm invisible.

I want to be seen,

I want to be heard,

or not.

I want to speak,

I want to choose,

or not,

things that matter to me —

not those arbitrarily determined for me,

by a body,

by a mind that is taking away my reasoning.

My choice, my voice.

I want to be normal.

I want to be me,

the real me.

No one explaining,

or speaking for me –

because of barriers perceived or real,

no distinguishing features

that reveal the person I am not.

I want to move about

in the day and night imperceptibly.

Not on anyone's radar.

I'm just there.

Because I want to be there,

not because *it* has taken me there.

I want to be normal.

I want to be me,

the real me...

Skyline in Philadelphia, Pa.

You've Got to Believe

If you want to fulfill dreams,

you've got to dream.

If you want to go forward

with your life,

you've got to take the first step.

Before you pronounce

what you're going to do to others,

proclaim it to yourself –

and believe you can do it.

Because you can.

III. Family

Fond Memories

There is a place,

a very special place

where I go whenever I want.

In my heart, and in my mind

I keep fond memories of those I've loved,

and those who have loved me.

Some have moved on, ahead of me.

Yet they are never far away

as I recall splendid moments,

times shared, and lives well lived.

I am truly thankful for these fond memories

forever and a day.

Oh! So Beautiful The Spot

Photograph and comments by my father,
Alfred A. Creveling

Family Album*

Bought at a flea market

a family album

with old photographs on brown pages

brought forward in time

by exchanging money.

I turned the pages

and wondered about

the people dressed so properly

who posed for a photograph

intending to capture

a moment in time now far removed.

No one to talk to,

to ask questions,

or seek answers to my queries.

No dates, names, times, or places

only faces,

props with no traces

black and white pictures

now fading and aging.

I closed the family album,

saddened in knowing

there was no one to remember

these people who lived

so very long ago.

*Influenced by a black-and-white photo album purchased in 1988

Alfred A. Creveling

Our Time Here is a Gift

I'm increasingly aware

our time here is not to be squandered

or taken lightly.

Today is a gift we have been given

to live in the knowledge

and with the challenge

of being fully alive

and emboldened to fulfill

all that we already are.

A Life in Review —
My Great-Grandfather

More than 100 years ago,

my father's father, my great-grandfather

lived upon the earth.

I read in the 1876 family Bible,

the one that was passed on to me

more than 50 years ago,

that he was a resilient and resourceful man.

Various times throughout the years

I've held this family heirloom in my hands.

Each time I picked it up

I was reminded of the many stories told.

It tells of my ancestors and their families,

most of whom have long ago departed.

Like a good custodian,

it's been my responsibility

to assure its safekeeping,

as it will be for my children,

and their children eventually.

Before there were photographs

there were lithographs.

There is one in this book, just one.

It is an image

of my great-grandfather.

I like to think I look a lot like him,

although I'm not sure I want those large ears

as I grow older.

This voluminous collection of history

is beautifully bound and illustrated,

with an ornamental design,

the kind you possibly have seen

on the *Antiques Roadshow.*

I have no interest in its monetary value.

It has never been about that for me.

This book has been a remarkable gift,

a blessing, to have all these years.

It's prompted me to think about the passage of time

and how quickly we move from the present

to a historical reference of years gone by.

Today, I thought of you,

my great-grandfather.

Thankful you lived and gave life to a son,

who gave life to a son,

who gave life to me.

Just as I've given life

to three sons and a daughter.

The Gathering

Our dining room table and chairs

have been donated to the Salvation Army.

We hope they will be discovered and used again.

We've yet to decide what to put in their place.

Lately, we've talked of buying a recliner

that would fill the space.

We have many fond memories

of family and friends sitting around the table,

sharing stories of special moments worth repeating.

There were times we dined by candlelight,

with fine linen, silverware,

and floral arrangements bright and pleasing.

It was our tradition before meals

to hold hands

as we each took our turn

and shared in giving thanks

for what we believed

to be our blessings

at that moment in time.

Of all the things we did at the table,

this, I believe I loved the most.

Epicurean delights often competed

with our desire for conversation.

Occasionally, there were those

who didn't know if they enjoyed eating

more than conversing

and spoke with mouths full

to say what they were thinking.

No wine connoisseurs

did anyone profess to be.

Creatively drawn labels on bottles

often determined our preferences

for the red or white we drank.

We didn't rush

to push ourselves

away from the table.

Sometimes we lingered

and wanted more of being together.

We laughed uninhibitedly

as we listened to many a fable.

No one was ever banished

from our table

because of political discourse

or differences of opinion

although occasionally,

reticence prevailed

as someone expressed a contrary view.

There were those

who spoke with great elocution

and a few who held forth

like they were in court.

Perhaps some may have even thought

of themselves as exceptional orators.

I miss our table and chairs,

this special gathering place.

Its absence

has made it abundantly clear

how blessed and fortunate we were

to engage in conversations

that challenged our thinking,

and often reminded us

of what life is really about.

Florence, Italy

Grandmother

My grandmother was the one

who showed us

how to live in faith.

"God is good.

He has a plan for all of us," she would say.

She never wavered,

doubted, or questioned:

"Why me, Lord, what have I done?"

She lived as she believed God intended her to,

every day, in every way in all that she did.

Sometimes I do wonder why,

and at times I don't understand God's master plan.

When in my faith I waver,

I think of her.

Resolute and determined.

A believer.

Although she's been gone now for many years,

I can still hear her talking to me

"Johnny," (that's what she called me)

"God loves you.

Don't you ever forget that!

If He can keep His eye on the sparrow,

that little bird,

certainly He has His eyes on you."

The way she said it, I believed.

Father

You were a good father.

That we know.

Honest, giving, and caring.

You often exclaimed it was your family

that was most important to you.

You never hesitated to express your view

on things in life that mattered to you.

There were times some of us wished

you had been a little less forthcoming about

telling others what to do.

You loved poetry and always had a favorite verse to share.

Frequently, you quoted a favorite poet:

Wordsworth, Keating, Lawrence, and Frost, to name a few.

Sometimes, too, we heard your own poems.

There were times I tuned you out.

Now, I wish I could remember and recite just one.

People who knew you have told me

I look a lot like you.

When I see my face in the mirror

I'm aware of the resemblance,

especially now that I'm older and I'm okay with that.

I can still picture you at your desk

with that ever-present jewel loupe firmly in place,

hunched over someone's hand-me-down watch

painstakingly restoring its ancient inner workings.

Although there were times you were frustrated,

you always finished what you started.

You never hesitated to show us your strength,

pulling yourself up with your fingers over a doorway.

We watched in amazement,

knowing we could never do that,

even though we were much younger!

You loved nature and often when we walked

the hills and countryside of our ancestors,

you told us of your faith in a higher power.

"He created the beauty that surrounds us,"

you would say.

No doubt He was with you

when you lovingly planted flowers

or tended gardens for friends and family.

You did all these things with your own money,

never asking or expecting to be paid.

It was your way of leaving a little of you behind.

You loved your family and we loved you back.

Although I'm not sure we told you enough.

Did You Know?

Did you know before you left us,
before forever, before you went away,
what it was you wanted to say?
When was it you felt
there would be no more chances,
no last minute awakening to share feelings,
emotions you rarely expressed?
What was it you wanted
and hoped would occur between you and me?
I'm still working through what was left unsaid.
Was there ever a moment when you knew
what it was you wanted to say?
Those years of reticence took their toll,
there is no denying that.
The emotions stirred—
were they there in the beginning
when you first held me?
I know you told me
but I don't remember all those years ago.
I really wish I could.
Now gone forever
chances for us to be together.
I don't believe I told you,
when I was growing up
that I love you, Dad.

Shattered Hopes and Dreams

I remember it well

although I wish I didn't.

When he would run into the night

seeking darkness to elude revealing the pain he was feeling.

It wasn't always that way.

There once was a time when he opened up his heart,

and offered it to her,

the woman he really loved,

the one who would become my mother.

I know this because of what I uncovered,

many years ago when he died.

A card he created expressly for her,

at a time when their relationship was fresh,

and filled with hope, joy,

and visions of a future together.

He professed his everlasting devotion

and would tell her that she was the one

he didn't want to get away

when they exchanged their vows all those years ago.

His intentions were pure

and he meant what he said

when he wrote in that card

"Your Adoring Husband."

She was the one

he would love, only her,

in sickness and health,

good times and hard times,

forever.

He promised he would be there for her.

Together, they would have five children,

three girls, and two boys.

My remembrance is that of a little boy,

when my father's hopes and dreams

were shattered and in disarray.

His spirit broken,

when he knew it was really over.

He would never recover

or begin anew with another,

that was not his style.

He truly loved her.

There would never be another for him,

my dad.

A Daughter's Gift

With a stroke of your fingers
you pushed aside the hair
that had fallen upon your face,
revealing your blue eyes.
Looked into mine
as I extended my arm
and offered you my hand.
This indeed was a special moment,
our first dance.
With your engaging smile
and unbridled enthusiasm,
you readily accepted,
stepped up,
and placed your feet upon mine.
The music played and thus we began,
and took those first dance steps together.
Step, step, step.
Step, step, step.
At the time, I thought I was showing you.
As I think about it now,
I realize that wasn't really true at all.
I had forgotten, and without knowing,
you were the one providing me
those wonderful lessons.
Ones that can never be replaced

by plastic cards and fancy clothes.

Nor faded blue jeans, new cars,

or big houses on the hill.

Things that conceal,

rather than reveal

who we truly are.

I cherish and hold in my heart

and will never part,

with the fond memories of those days.

When a little girl gave to her daddy,

innocence, eagerness,

and unequivocal love.

Really, the greatest gift of all.

John P. Creveling

From Dad to You

There were times as your dad
when I didn't always get it right.
Didn't do,
didn't say,
what I should have.
For that I'm truly sorry.
Too late for excuses,
I surely regret
those times I wasn't there for you.
Missed opportunities
in being your dad,
to be by your side.
Holding your hand a little longer
before you grew up.
Crossing a street,
when it should have been me
looking out for you.
We did have special moments between us,
times I do remember well
when I did get it right
and we didn't rush our being together.
Of course, I wish now
we had had a whole lot more of those occasions
when it was just you and me.
Those moments certainly were memorable to me.

I hope they were for you as well.

In all these years,

I've never regretted being your dad.

The regrets I have are of me, not you.

I love you.

I always have, and of course,

I always will.

Dad

More Than a Picture

Your picture still hangs on the wall,

all by itself.

I wanted to take it down,

but each time I tried

I saw your face looking back at me.

It's still there,

right where I put it

all those many years ago.

My memories, too,

of our days together

are vivid, and fresh.

How could I ever forget you?

You're still in my heart.

In all the time I knew you,

you never once wavered.

Your love was unconditional.

There were times when I held back,

and was unavailable,

yet that didn't seem to matter to you,

that was not your style.

You were a gift from God to me.

My companion all those years ago.

I hold on to my memories

of when you were here,

our lives together,

of what was once good and beautiful.

You were so much more than a pet.

You were my best friend.

I miss you.

John P. Creveling

Wish I Could Remember It All

I remember,

but I don't remember it all.

Days of my youth

and those times we played in the park.

Was it you who said

we'd always have these memories,

or was it me?

Now that you are gone,

I'd like to have

some of those lost memories

of living our days

in splendid ways

with me now.

Hope, Jeff, and Chris Robertson

Istanbul, Turkey

Venice, Italy

Angkor Wat, Cambodia

Machu Picchu, Peru

IV. Love

Bridal shop display and
reflection in window, Paris

First Kiss

I don't recall when it was
I first discovered love.
I have no clear image
of one girl,
or a special occasion
when that might have taken place.
It's my first kiss I recall,
and the girl
who wondered, as I did,
what it was all about.
We both were 12,
eager to be teenagers,
moving us closer
toward adolescence.
I wish I could remember her name.
I really do.
Perhaps,
if I think more about her
and less on what we did that day,
I will recall the name of the girl
who negotiated our first kiss.
From my house

by way of the crow,

walking through the fields,

she lived less than a half-mile away.

Although we took a different path to school,

we shared the same homeroom

and knew many of the same kids.

Some were my friends,

many were hers,

she was a popular girl as I recall.

We sat together on the ground that day.

Not far away,

the community pool

was being filled with spring water.

In the days that followed,

the gates were opened

and testosterone

pushed forward

as young boys en masse

asserted territorial rights

for ground to be occupied,

however briefly, each day.

We looked at each other,

giggling as young boys and girls do,

when she said to me,

"Do you want to kiss?"

I know it wasn't me

who offered to kiss.

At the time,

I was really shy around girls

and lacked the courage

to ask for what I wanted.

There was no reluctance

as we both enthusiastically said, "Yes."

We would kiss for the very first time.

Yet, sitting there we knew

neither one of us had a clue

how we should proceed.

She cheerfully suggested

that we count to three

which I eagerly said I would do.

I took a deep breath

and quickly blurted out, "1, 2, 3."

It was her nose I kissed

as my eyes had been closed

when I went for her lips.

My face must have been vivid red.

Fortunately, for me,

she was a mature 12-year-old girl.

She looked at me, smiled, and said

she wasn't ready.

Simple as that.

I would get to do it again.

So we agreed to count to three *together*,

and to kiss on our lips,

just in case *I* was uncertain

as to where I should place my first kiss.

Looking in each other's eyes,

the count began,

"1, 2, (a long pause between 2 and 3—she was teasing me) 3."

We both moved forward, slowly,

each with our eyes wide open,

touching our lips,

just enough,

that we both agreed to do it again,

and again.

There you have it.

Now you know,

it was she,

that nameless girl,

not me,

who proffered what was our first kiss.

The one I remember from all those years ago.

John P. Creveling

When Was It You Knew?

When was it you knew

that I was the one?

Was it when your heart skipped a beat,

took a deep breath,

and held on to it—yearningly?

In that moment,

you knew,

you knew,

that I was the one for you.

There would be no other.

Was it the moment that I knew?

When my heart skipped a beat?

When I took a deep breath,

and held on to it longingly?

I had no doubt

you were the one for me.

There could be no other,

or would be,

ever again for me.

Lady Christina

There was a moment in the middle of the night

when I awoke from a bad dream,

seeking desperately to know

that I was alive in the world.

In that moment of being aware

while you lay soundly sleeping

I reached out to touch you

not to wake you

just to know you were alright.

Felt your pulse and listened to your heartbeat.

Without realizing it, we began to breathe in unison.

In that moment, it was as if we were one.

I found comfort being there with you.

As I closed my eyes,

I quickly began dreaming anew

of all things wonderful and beautiful, thanks to you.

Unabashed Love

Lay down upon the living room floor last night
with my loved one.
It was just the two of us.
That's the place we wanted to be.
We weren't seeking redemption,
we were mutual provocateurs.
She held me and I held her,
we didn't need words
to express what we were feeling.
There was nothing we were concealing
only revealing
as we sought a different kind of healing.
There was no complexity
in what we wanted for each other.
Unencumbered by any expectations,
we let our spirits soar
and discovered new highs,
beyond any we could have imagined.

Dance of Love

I want to hold you in my arms,

and dance our dance,

the one where we close our eyes,

mindful of no other,

it's just you and me,

as it was the very first time.

We hear the music,

and fill the space

with moves we've created.

No fixed nor orchestrated steps,

our body, our feet

respond to each other's emotions.

The joy that we feel

in that unique moment

keeps us present

to the now that we have,

and the realization,

that's all anyone has.

May I have this dance?

I want to hold you in my arms,

and dance our dance,

The one where we close our eyes mindful of no other…

John P. Creveling

The One You Hold to Your Chest

This passion we've known,

we wish never to end.

Not to be forgotten or wasted.

Never to forget the warmth,

the smile, and radiant face

of the one you hold close.

It's the voice we hear in our heads

that reminds us how precious and wonderful

life really is

when you are with the one you love.

Wedding Day

Expressions of Love

I love those moments

when we walk together

holding hands.

Our pace is simple,

we pick our feet up

and put them back down.

We may notice our surroundings,

or not.

Hear the bird sing its song of joy

amidst the noise.

Talk of life, living,

of our yesterdays,

and our tomorrows,

and the quickness of time passing.

Holding your hand in mine,

I feel your warmth

of which I never tire.

Our hands may have changed

and reveal our aging,

but my heart always beats

a little faster when I'm with you.

It's by No Accident

The years have gone by rapidly

of that we have no doubt.

Still we may wonder

how is it we find ourselves here,

together, these many years later.

We have not delayed

the significance of each new day

as we rose

well before many mornings' light.

We savor our days

as we experience the fullness and richness

we've come to know and love

living in our moments.

By no accident,

we've discovered

within ourselves

the spirit that gives us

the courage to dream

and believe in ourselves.

We have been blessed

with an abundance

of joy, beauty, laughter,

friendship, curiosity,

awe, and wonder.

I cherish each day

I have with you.

Truly thankful

for the gift of love

you've given me.

This one's for you,

and you know it's true,

I love you.

Happy Threesome!
James, You, and Me
(Caution/Warning: R Rated
May not be Suitable for Under-Aged Children)

Girl, you're looking sexy,

burning up the floor

dancing to our favorite music.

Let's turn off the lights,

burn some candles,

close the windows,

and pull down the shades.

I know it doesn't matter to you,

you're such a free spirit

and I'm such a private person.

But I'd rather no one

hear or see

what's going on

inside these walls.

I know what it can be like

when James gets into our head.

How many years has it been

since the very first time

we realized we wanted each other?

Tore off all our clothes

and left them right there,

in plain sight,

all scattered about.

There was no doubt where we were going,

the trail was one way,

there was no going back.

We were high,

and it wasn't from smoking.

It was just you and me.

Well, there was James.

He was there with us

from the beginning.

Good thing I'm not jealous,

of this threesome.

James Taylor, you, and me,

alone with his music and lyrics.

Wow, what a great song,

Your Smiling Face.

Sometimes I can't get it out of my head,

especially when I think about

the places it takes us to.

I wonder what he'd say,

if he knew how many times

his song found its way

into our lives.

It's the one song

that never fails

to get some action going.

We let go of our inhibitions,

even set aside life's challenges,

no need to bring unnecessary luggage with us.

I like it when we go there,

to our special place,

the one we share,

even if it is a threesome,

James, you, and me.

My Friend

You and me,

we could talk about anything,

there was nothing off limits.

We didn't need a blood connection.

We were the best of friends.

Perhaps closer than a brother or sister.

There were times we finished a sentence

the other had started.

Times, too, when I was wondering how you were,

what you were doing at that particular moment.

A few minutes later, the phone would ring,

it was you.

I wanted to pick up the telephone and call you today.

Just as I had done so many times before.

The sunrise I saw looking out my window

left me breathless.

I wanted to share it with you.

For a moment,

I forgot.

My Love for You is Real

I wish I could articulate

how it is I feel.

Although there never is a moment

that is ideal.

At times our love seems surreal.

I don't want to conceal,

I'd rather get down and kneel

and reveal

how my love for you is real.

This Old House

There are times when I linger in bed.

I do not rush to begin the new day or end the old.

With my eyes closed

I listen to the settled sounds our house makes.

The crackling of its old wood,

the floor boards expanding and contracting

as if someone were walking upon them.

Perhaps someone is,

this is, after all, an old house with a history of its own.

It was first documented in the 1860

American census.

In this very house,

that originally had two stories,

five families lived.

Among them were a seamstress,

a blacksmith, a maid, and a cook.

They were people of color who most

likely served

the much larger homes on more

prestigious streets,

like Delancey and Pine.

This house was fresh and new in 1860,

the same year Abraham Lincoln was elected president.

The American Civil War had not yet begun,

and the Gettysburg address wouldn't be read

for another three years.

There was no telephone,

it hadn't yet been invented.

That wouldn't occur for another 16 years, in 1876.

This house has been home to generations.

Although I'm uncertain who they were,

I've often thought about those

who have preceded us in living here.

Christina H. Robertson ©2018

Were they married or single?

Did they discover love

and shout out into the night,

mindful of each other

while oblivious to anyone else?

No doubt there were those

conceived here,

some who were born here,

and possibly, too,

those who died here.

Did they have faith in a God

or no faith at all?

Had they lost their beliefs

to a country divided?

The original fireplace is still here

the one we've used for a romantic mood,

rather than its intended function

of providing warmth on cold days and nights.

It's a house that was built

on a stone foundation,

mortar and brick hold it solidly together.

Its walls I imagine have been painted over

with each new owner

wanting to make it uniquely their own.

Its plasterwork has blemishes,

which I generously refer to as "character."

For more than a quarter of a century,

we've lived here.

Filled these walls

with an abundance of laughter,

hosted countless parties,

and shared conversations.

Held no malice

toward others

when we debated politics

of differing views and opinions.

We've nurtured

our love for each other in this house.

There were times when we planned our future here.

Now, we talk of growing old.

Soon a time will come

when it's our turn to leave,

I will do so reluctantly.

Like those before us

and those that follow,

we hope we've been good custodians.

Just maybe,

we've left some memories here.

I sure hope we have.

My drawing of the Betsy Ross House,
Philadelphia, Pa.

There with You

Central Highlands, Scotland

I'd like to be there with you

when the sun comes up,

to see the new light of day.

We need not speak or express,

what it was we were seeing,

nor what it was we were feeling.

It would be enough to be there with you

in that moment together.

I'd like to be there with you

when the sun is setting

in the west,

at the end of the day.

91

I'd like to be there with you

to watch a full moon caress the earth.

To see its craters,

to see the man in the moon,

as we have done before.

Perhaps it will take us on a journey,

a journey of reflections.

Memories.

Life.

The life we've lived.

The times we've known.

We need no one to remind us

how incredibly blessed we have been.

We know.

We've lived it.

Every day in every way.

We lived.

I'd like to be there with you

at the end of our days,

together into eternity.

V. Heroes

Heroes

I've been thinking lately of heroes.

Not people whose names we've heard,

or are readily recognizable.

The names of my heroes will never appear

on a movie marque.

Yet, they deserve to be there.

They are the real "stars"

of our society.

Lifelike images of them

will not be printed

on any currency.

No statues dedicated,

or historic postage stamps

depicting them at a favorable time in life.

They are noble.

My Parents

Yet, they do not seek nobility,

or recognition for their deeds

as they show us all the value of humility.

They are refreshingly earnest in their endeavors,

not wanting to defame, denigrate,

or use excessive vulgarity to draw attention to themselves.

They provide us with much needed sobriety.

They personify individuals

worthy of emulation as they live their lives

in civility and integrity.

They may struggle at times, miss a step, stumble,

and occasionally benefit from a helping hand.

Yet, they are steadfast and unwavering

in their determination to provide for themselves

and their families

a solid foundation built with hope, love,

empathy, and faith. They wish a better tomorrow for all.

The real heroes of this age or any age

are our mothers, fathers, sons, daughters,

friends, and neighbors.

Those unnamed and unknown workers

who labor behind the scenes,

people we've never met.

The ones working while we are sleeping.

Individuals we barely notice

in our streets and neighborhoods.

If there is a "Golden Book,"

surely their names will be written boldly upon it.

These are the people of our country,

who are the true heroes.

More Than What You See

There are times
when I may falter and stumble,
and some say I even mumble.
It's not that I do it intentionally,
it just happens that way
without my consent.
Sometimes, too, my body
involuntarily moves without
my wanting it to,
and I seem to be flailing.
This, I have no desire to do either.
You need only know
this to be true,
I'm so much more
than what you see.
You see what is obvious,
readily visible and exposed –
my vulnerability.
I know what's on the inside
may not always be available to you.
I confess I don't like to grumble,
nor do I want to make much of a hullabaloo.
That's really not my style,
although at times,
my wife thinks I'm into denial.

Salvador, Brazil

96

If you were to ask her,

she will also tell you

she believes me to be an optimist,

even an idealist, and

a dreamer of what can be.

Call me an optimist.

Call me an idealist.

Call me, too, a dreamer.

I will readily admit

I am all of these and more.

I dream there will come a day,

a time when we can vanquish

all the diseases that we have known

once and for all!

No more Parkinson's disease,

cancer, MS, or dementia.

They'll all be gone.

Until that time comes,

I say to you,

avert your eyes

from the obvious,

if only for a brief moment.

Possibly then

your focus will be

on what really matters,

what's in a person's heart

for I'm more than what you see!

John P. Creveling

Eagle's Lament*

Above me the eagle flies noble in flight

with boundless strength and energy,

seeing much more than I.

Undaunted by the wind,

yet he struggles to survive.

America's symbol

of Peace and War

for more than ten score

beckons to be free

of legend and myth

to soar once more,

as before,

its numbers in abundance

to journey free.

*Written July 4, 1986

In Celebration of Muhammad Ali

We had a kinship,

Muhammad Ali and me.

Although he never knew it,

he was my brother.

Not of blood,

but of faith and fortitude.

In all things,

he celebrated life.

A pugnacious fighter,

in and out of the ring.

He walked tall and proud

and proclaimed himself to be "The Greatest."

Ultimately we believed he was.

Charismatic and self-assured,

he had a disarming smile

and an irrepressible twinkle in his eye.

He spoke eloquently and poetically.

His voice and words

inspired millions of people worldwide.

I was one of them.

Many years after he retired

from the boxing sport which he had re-energized,

he would once again

enter the arena as an Olympian.

Out of the darkness

he courageously and hauntingly

stepped into the light once more.

Like a knight he bravely carried the torch

that would light the caldron

of the Games of the XXVI Olympiad.

His biggest competition of his life

had come from within,

he knew that more than anyone else.

That day in 1996

the world saw his struggle to walk forward,

his brave face

and what we knew to be his remarkable determination.

Muhammad Ali was a hero

to legions of people throughout the world.

Rightfully so.

He was one of mine.

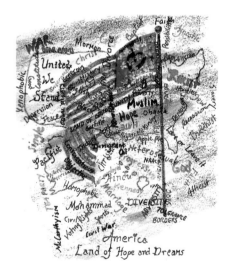

God's Gift—An Angel on Earth
Written for Mattie Stepanek

When I look up into the sky

and see the stars at night

I often think of you

and wonder where you are.

Surely you are there,

a new star, shining brightly in the heavens

for all the universe to see.

While in this world you were a beacon,

you gave us all hope and inspiration.

Your heart was open,

for you shared your love liberally and completely.

Confronted with obstacles and challenges,

when the best of us would have questioned,

"Why me, Lord?"

You responded, "Why not me?"

You showed us one and all how to live,

and ultimately, how to die.

Surely God himself gave us this angel on earth,

in the ravaged body of a small boy.

Your time on earth was brief.

Yet, in your 13 years of living,

you never once equivocated.

"After the storm there is light," you said.

Sometimes, we just have to find it for ourselves.

When we do, we begin to understand

how big your heart really was.

The angel you were here on earth,

and the one you are now,

from above.

The Wall

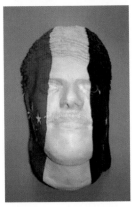

I've never been able
to just *look* at "The Wall,"
or simply walk by.
I, who am alive,
acknowledge those I once knew,
among the 58,282 names etched in stone.
Faces and names I promised myself
I would never forget, but I have.

They were dreamers, too, everyone
who dreamt of love, marriage,
children, and family.
They had aspirations, ideals, and ambitions
never to be attained.
When we were kids, my cousin, Danny, and I
liked to imagine we were musketeers.
Never far from home
we would run in the fields,
up and down the hills into the valleys,
off to rescue damsels in distress.
Danny's name is there, etched for eternity.
His son never to know his father.
A father never to know he had a son.
I pause at this sacred place,
The Wall.
I bow my head,

close my eyes,

and always,

always, honor,

and keep in my heart,

those once young,

who lived as we do now.

Once ordinary,

now heroes all.

I wish they weren't.

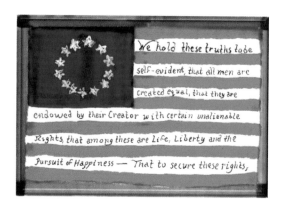

VI. God and Spirituality

Valley of the Kings, Egypt

105

I Know Where I'm Going

I know where I've been

and I know where I'm going.

I know I never need to walk alone.

The God I know

is the one who was there in the beginning.

There is no secret to living.

He has told us so.

I know where I've been

and where I'm going,

in spite of myself.

Wheel at the base of the
Eiffel Tower, Paris

Phantom Writer

Somewhere from deep within,
unexpectedly a reservoir of words emerges
I didn't know was there.
Before it flies away,
vanishes, or comes in disarray,
I quickly replay in my mind without delay
these golden words
I've been inspired to write today.
Although sometimes I may hesitate
and wonder,
did I get it right
or, will it require a rewrite?
Like a bundle of flowers
when skillfully arranged
reveals the inherent beauty
which few are able to see
until it becomes a bouquet,
a rainbow of colors
that takes our breath away.
There are times when
my heart takes precedence
and propels me to express
emotions evoking
words of love, beauty,
and tenderness.

Sometimes, too,

an economy of words

is all I need to say succinctly,

what otherwise

I've been struggling to convey.

It can be magical, or mystical,

and sometimes unequalled and magnificent.

It's as if I were describing the

quest for the pot of gold

at the end of the rainbow.

Whatever I've written,

I hope it resonates with you

as much as it has for me.

Through it all,

'tis my good fortune to be able to say

the sentiments expressed come from my heart,

and that's always a good place to start.

Montezuma's Castle, Arizona

Embrace Me

You watched over me,

fed and clothed me when I was not able.

Gave me shelter, nurtured, and comforted me.

When I could not walk, you picked me up

and carried me.

Loved me

and gave me hope when I needed it the most.

Lit the path when I could not see.

Brought me out of darkness into the light.

Now I'm able and I hope I'll provide

the same to others when they, too,

need it the most.

God Knows

In Sunday school, our teacher told us,
"God knows, God knows, God knows all.
Everything. No hiding from him.
He is omnipotent."
I remember it all.
There in that sacred space believing it all.
She told us,
"He died for you and me."
We accepted Him into our lives.
He sat at our tables,
we talked to Him daily.
He knew each one of us by name.
He would be there for you and me
in our time of need.
We were young and innocent,
we wanted to believe,
and we did,
we believed it all.
With faith in God a chosen few
learned how to kill and went off to war
far away from home believing it all.
Forevermore lives altered,
shattered, and severed.
Many came back, many did not.
Names now indelibly etched on a wall.

Each name carries its own weight

of lost loved ones remembered.

Centuries from now, I wonder, if anyone will care

and say a prayer for those who died in wars, far from home.

I speak to god* still,

in my own way.

Our relationship has inexorably changed.

As if to underscore the difference,

I may not call upon him daily,

I sometimes forget.

*Lowercase intentional to suggest a shift in relationship.

Hands of God, Rodin, Paris

John P. Creveling

You Are Not Alone—You Are Loved

Have you ever seen an indigo sky,

one that left you breathless?

You groped for air

as you searched for words,

but none could be found

to give voice to that gift before you.

The spectacle awoke such awe

you wanted to take a picture

or wished you could paint

like Vincent Van Gogh.

That moment you wished,

you hoped,

to keep in your heart and mind forever.

That day. That sky.

You saw, you noticed,

what surely had been created

by the master himself.

It was His gift to us all.

But you took the time to see it.

Alight your spirit,

take flight.

Know that in all the days before,

and all those that follow,

You are not alone.

You are loved.

My Prayer

In my own way
to God I pray
each and every day.
While here
in this world
let me be present
to moments of now, today.
In my living,
I stay above the fray,
and do not contribute in any way
to times of discord
or disarray.
My voice,
my words encourage harmony
and unite people,
rather than contribute toward discord
that inflame and ignite.
This journey,
this path I walk,
let me shine light
on what I believe to be right,
regardless of the distance.
I know well,
things aren't always black and white,
and might doesn't make right.

Sometimes we may need to be contrite.

Allow me to listen,

and be patient,

before I rush into decisions

without having full knowledge.

Give me the wisdom to grasp

and discern

right from wrong

in spite of what might be popular.

I do what is right

even if I must stand alone.

My one life

while in this world

has positive meaning,

influence, and impact

for the time I am here.

This is my prayer to God

and to myself.

Hey Jesus

Hey Jesus, it's me, your child.

I'm calling.

Hope I don't need an appointment.

I know it's been a while since we've talked.

Just in case you haven't noticed,

the world's in disarray, war still goin' on,

innocent people being killed.

It's called "collateral damage."

What happened to love and peace?

Why can't we all just get along?

Politicians lying to us, makin' promises

just to get elected and reelected.

Hey Jesus, it's me. I'm calling.

Hope I don't need an appointment.

I just took the Bible down from the shelf and dusted it off.

Can't understand with a world of such abundance

why so many people are without food and water,

starving and dying.

When will we learn the power within?

All things are possible to those who believe,

we need not wait for a second coming.

Hey Jesus, it's me. I'm calling.

Hope you're listening,

because we need some help today.

A little guidance with the master plan.

John P. Creveling

Were You There, Lord?

Were you there with me, Lord,
when I took my first breath,
my first step?
When my parents first held me
in their arms?
Did you know, Lord,
what I'd do through the years,
if you saw my potential,
what my life would be about?
Were you there, Lord,
when my first child
came into existence,
when he, too,
took his first breath,
his first step?
Was it you, Lord
who intervened
and saved the life
of my son, John,
a little boy who couldn't have known
he was drinking turpentine?
Sometimes I pray, Lord,
sometimes I wonder.
Were you there, Lord
when John Kennedy died in Dallas,

Martin Luther King in Memphis,

and Bobby in Los Angeles?

I'd like to say I know,

I wish I could say it were so.

I've yet to understand, Lord,

I wish it were true.

I'd like to say I know.

Notre Dame Cathedral, Paris

An Old 45

There are times when music is playing in my head.

Tunes I readily recognize and I sing along.

I sound pretty good if I must say so myself,

especially when it's all in my mind

and there is no one listening

to act like a critic.

Sometimes like an old 45 record

with the needle stuck in a groove,

these songs repeat themselves

just for me.

And then there are those

where I don't recall the words,

just the melody,

and I simply hum along.

Those songs I recall

set me in motion and I start to tap my feet,

clap my hands,

and begin rhythmically moving my body

as the music has its way with me.

If you should see me

at a time when the music is playing in my head,

feel free to dance along.

Who cares if other people might think of us

as being a little crazy?

Does it really matter?

There once was a time

all those many years ago

when people proclaimed

"Rock n Roll is the devil's music."

Yet here we are today,

somehow we all survived.

The world didn't come to an end

and Satan hasn't possessed

anyone I know lately.

Cape Town, South Africa

John P. Creveling

Always with Me

In this body I have abided
for more than three score.
I've lived moments of sheer delight
and profound enlightenment.
Fulfilled dreams imagined
and those not thought possible.
I've known occasions of sadness,
yet have chosen not to dwell there.
With my eyes wide open,
I've seen unveiled beauty
where others had been blind.
Lived times in my life
when I thought I walked alone.
But that's not really true
as I think about you.
You were always with me.

Love and Grace

I dreamt last night I was welcomed

to visit a special place,

unlike any I have ever seen.

There was no darkness or night,

only glorious colors throughout.

While my surroundings

were not intimately familiar

I felt considerable comfort in being there.

I was shown a book,

the size, weight, and beauty

of which I'd never seen before.

Great care had been taken

to write upon its pages

names of people chosen

for a future journey, not near, not far.

I felt like a voyeur and uncertain

and wondered why I was there.

Someone with an angelic voice,

neither male nor female,

whispered in my ear:

"All will be made clear

when your time is near.

Do not despair,

there are many

who love you here."

When in the morning

I awoke, upon my cheek

I realized

a single tear

had settled there.

Should I forget

and ever feel

absence of hope,

I know to touch my face.

It is there.

It reminds me of love and grace.

Paris, France

Let Us Speak of the Unspoken

I'm a bit reluctant to admit this,

for it's not one of my better moments.

Yet I believe it's a story sadly repeated

by many more than just me.

There have been times

when I averted my eyes

because I did not want to see

those who were in need

of more than I was willing to acknowledge.

I am not proud to say

there have been times

when I've even taken a different path

and walked around those downtrodden people.

Occupied my mind with other things,

to divert my thoughts

from what was really there before me.

Deceptions, illusions,

keeping an arm's length

will not make it different.

They will not fade away.

They really do exist.

They live among us,

in our streets,

and in our communities.

Those without shelter,

food, and adequate clothing,

whose faces we avoid most days.

No quick-fix solutions

have provided resolution

to their plight.

As we pray to God tonight,

all snuggled in our bed

feeling quite secure,

just before going off to sleep,

let us speak of compassion,

forgiveness,

and love

for all.

My Time on Earth

No one knows

except perhaps my God

and me,

sometimes I lie awake

in the middle of the night.

I doubt you'd guess what it's about.

I certainly wish for

all to be well in the world.

An end to poverty and deprivation,

no one wanting for shelter,

everyone to have a full stomach,

for more than one day.

Yes, too,

I wish we all could see

and know a time of peace

throughout the world.

I laugh as I acknowledge this now,

for as you read this,

you might think it frivolous of me,

and possibly a little selfish for what I'm about to say.

I ask God not to be famous,

nor my name be readily recognizable.

But that my life be of value

that I have a positive impact with the journey I am on

and that this voice, the one that is mine,

and the skills I've undertaken to learn

be applied purposely and not wasted.

Though our time on earth is short,

I remember to evoke humor in my living

and not forget what Oscar Wilde said all those years ago,

"Life is too important to be taken seriously."

I fill my life with laughter and spontaneity,

joy, and, of course, love.

Let the Light in—Release the Darkness

I pulled on the shade in my window

so that I might release it

and let the light in,

so I could see.

When I did

the light shone upon the darkness

and I wondered,

was I ready for its unveiling

and what it might uncover?

Have I Achieved
All You Thought I Would?

There are times I wonder who it was

that made me who I am.

Was it you?

You've been here a long time.

Did you have your say

about the person I've become?

My grandmother often talked of a higher power,

one who is all-knowing and supreme.

She would say

in spite of ourselves,

you would always care,

and we should never lose hope,

you loved everyone.

In all these years I've lived,

have I achieved all you thought I would?

Did I get it right?

Have I fulfilled the dream you had for me?

Surely there were times I faltered,

had my share of false starts,

and even took a few steps backward.

Did you ever doubt

I'd accomplish

all that you thought I would?

I don't believe

we'll get a second chance
to do it all over.
What life we have,
this is it.
Before I leave,
I hope I have fulfilled
all that you knew I could.

I've Arrived

It's amazing the things
that bothered me in the past
no longer seem
relevant in the present.
Life has occurred in between
and I've discovered
the joy and value of understanding that.

VII. Summing Up

This is me throughout the years – from 14 months old
to present day. (Collage by Christina H. Robertson ©2018)

If Not Now, When?

I don't know what will happen when I die,

once my heart stops beating and I've taken my last breath,

after my body collapses,

as my time on earth is ending,

no one can say for sure.

I hope I'll have time to say goodbye,

possibly share myself a little more,

and tell some of my stories,

especially those I believe worthy of repeating.

Tell those I love one more time,

I'm not sure I told them enough how really special

my life has been because they were in it.

At times, I have wondered if I did enough

with the skills and talents that were clearly mine,

I'm not sure I'll ever know.

Like the shifting of the wind,

there were times in my life I believed I wasted

on things of unimportance.

But as I look back on it now,

perhaps that was when I was learning the most,

going further than I imagined for myself.

Those moments I now can say

made me a better person along the way.

Pass It On!

If you have known great joy,

uncontrollable laughter, bewilderment, too,

embraced the child within,

lived with wonder,

used your imagination,

found ways to explore the world,

even if you never left home,

exhausted yourself trying and doing,

perhaps not always successful,

but you still followed your bliss,

your dreams of achieving great things

for yourself and others,

been loved and given love,

felt pain in your heart

as you've known loss,

howled at the full moon just because you wanted to,

or cried into the night

when no one else could hear you,

found friendship and compassion,

camped in a tent beside a lake.

If at night you viewed the celestial heavens,

saw a shooting star,

and wished upon it,

love, health, and happiness

for more than yourself,

if in the middle of a rainstorm

without hesitation you placed your umbrella

in the hands of another who did not have one,

you received much pleasure,

as you rediscovered the joy

of dancing in the rain once more,

paid for the meal of another

without their knowledge,

secretly hoping it would be paid forward,

rolled down the lawn

so that your grandchildren might follow

and experience spontaneous joy and laughter,

knowing full well you would go back into the house

to change your clothes before you headed off to work,

spoken for the unspoken,

volunteered in some fashion,

for more than a day in your life,

shared your knowledge by mentoring another,

learned to live without malice,

sang songs of joy and hope, even if off key,

prepared a meal for someone who didn't have,

played hopscotch past the age of 40,

made faces as you emulated the primates at the zoo,

held a baby in your arms,

put your head out the window

of a fast-moving vehicle,

just to feel the wind in your face,

sat on the beach

with your eyes closed and really listened,

as if for the very first time,

to the waves of the ocean crashing on the shore,

and felt your own heartbeat.

If you have done these things and more,

then, this one's expressly written for you—

Pass It On!

My drawing of Amsterdam

Sage

I've made my share of mistakes.
There is no hiding from that.
Faltered at times.
Done things I wish I hadn't.
Said things, too, I've regretted.
My life hasn't always been stellar.
If you know me at all,
you might even attest to that.
There were times in my life
when I heard voices.
Not in my head,
but of well-intended people,
offering their sage advice,
hoping I might avoid
repeating the same mistakes.
I believe they genuinely cared
about the person I was becoming.
Looking back,
it's easy for me to say
I wish I had listened.
Thinking I knew so much more,
I resisted.
I know now they were more right than wrong.
Yet, perhaps those times in my life when I struggled
was when I learned the most.

Those experiences made me stronger.

I learned the lessons I needed to learn,

making me the man I am today.

Now that I'm an elder,

I'd like to give you some advice...

Outside Cairo, Egypt

Age

That person in the mirror looking back at me,

I am intimately familiar with,

I've known him since birth.

What used to be little brown spots,

seem to have multiplied and appear everywhere.

Now that I've begun to notice,

I realize I've earned every one of them.

I have more sags than I recall.

They seem to have embraced me,

that's obvious to see.

My hair has stayed with me I'm able to say,

although now more white than the light brown it used to be.

My ears keep growing with the passage of each year.

Thank goodness, I can cover them

with the longer hair I now wear.

My vision hasn't been 20/20 for a long time,

and my need for glasses is becoming increasingly clear.

I'm unable to extend my arms far enough,

that I might read and see what is really not that far away.

Boy, I'm sure glad I looked in the mirror today.

My visions of youth and beauty left me a long time ago.

Certainly no delusions here.

Life's Choices

I've never been much

for standing in someone else's shadow,

following.

That's just not me.

It's my own heartbeat I've listened to

that has made the difference.

When to go, and when to hold back.

It's never been about *the road less traveled.*

I really don't mind walking on a path others have taken.

It's where it's going that matters to me.

I've realized an amazing number of my life's choices

and it hasn't always been because of me.

I've had help along the way.

How fortunate I am to be able to say that.

John P. Creveling

My Old Friend

How is it that the days, weeks, and months we've lived,

became years and decades so quickly?

Our fathers told us it would be so,

but we weren't ready to hear or listen.

We didn't want to believe it either.

Now *we know.*

It's just as they said:

"It all will go by so quickly,

faster than you ever imagined."

Wasn't it just yesterday

when you and I ventured into the woods

and revealed our innocence and vulnerability?

Unlike those who preceded us into the forest,

what was it we said we would do differently?

Something about not wasting our time or our youth.

We would value every new day.

Savor the years, too,

before we would be the ones looking back.

I seem to recall we took a pledge.

Crossed our hearts, pricked our fingers,

revealing our blood, as we held each other's pinkies,

and promised forever and a day,

we'd always be the best of friends.

I remember that day.

As I think about us,

the past is present with me now,

and I'm wondering where are you today?

I'm still here.

Are you as well?

Did you travel the world like you said you would?

Did you see the Taj Mahal in all its splendor?

Was it like the picture in our fourth grade history books?

Did you hike the trails into the mountains of Peru

and see Machu Picchu,

one of the seven wonders of the world?

Have you settled down and raised a family of your own?

Did you achieve all you proclaimed for yourself

that day so many years ago?

Did you become the person you said you wanted to be?

No more, no less my forever old friend,

I thought of you today.

Taj Mahal, India

In Dreams

When I sleep, I dream
and frequently take journeys
to near and faraway places.
Some seem intimately familiar,
as if I've been there before.
Many others are unknown to me.
Like an explorer I'm seeking adventure
and discovery of the unknown.
There are magical times, too,
in recurrent dreams when I take flight,
rising above mere mortal limitations.
I soar at my own pace.
I'm not pretending to be Superman.
I don't wear a red cape.
These are the times
I'm in no rush to awaken.
My imagination,
visions of travel in the sky
embolden me in the day,
revive my soul,
and my spirit.
I may not always recall
my dreams and what they were about.
Increasingly my world is filled
with more questions than answers.

I've opened my mind to the world of possibilities.

I believe that's a good place to be.

To wonder what life is,

and how I will live in the world,

how, too, I will be in the world.

Along the way,

I know I want to celebrate more frequently.

I've traveled far,

been to many places.

I've lived a good life.

It's been rich and full.

Real and imaginary.

Thailand

Time

In my youth,

there were occasions when

I foolishly wished

for time to go by quickly.

Couldn't wait to be 16,

18, 21, and even 30.

To grow up, to be an adult.

Even in times of great beauty

I was impatient.

I rushed spectacular sunsets,

the roaring ocean,

The beauty of silent snowfalls,

wanting time to pass

To deliver tomorrow.

My parents knowing much more than me would say

"Don't be in such a rush to grow up,

it will all happen soon enough."

They got it right.

Now that I'm much older,

I wish I could have some of that time back.

I'd spend more time with my children

being children.

On a rainy day,

playing in the rain,

finding the puddle,

and jumping into it,

rather than avoiding it.

It seemed to go by all-too-quickly.

I'd like to wave a magic wand

and slow it down a bit.

To gaze upon the stars a little longer.

Savor times with loved ones.

Share stories of living and lessons learned.

Those people that lived long ago,

did they, too,

wish for time to go faster in their youth,

and then get that time back as they were older?

Florence, Italy

Know This to Be True of Me

We know this to be true,

this life we have

will one day come to an end.

There will be no turning back,

it's as simple as that.

In case you've ever wondered about me

and this life I've lived,

I will readily acknowledge

I've made my share of mistakes – whoopers aplenty,

I truly regret and wish I hadn't.

I apologize, too,

to those I may have offended along the way

with my words and activities that were not forthright,

nor honest, and in true character

of the person I am today.

But, per chance you don't know this about me:

while in this world I lived!

I lived an astonishingly rich and full life

with a wealth of love, laughter, and adventure.

I've been fortunate to have had many friendships,

ones, too, of permanence and sustaining presence.

I've walked among giants,

not in their shadows,

but with them, and among them

as they lifted me up

when I needed it the most
and made me feel stronger
and even taller than I really was.
I've quickened my pace
while my heart beat faster
with my face in the wind fully awake,
knowing I was alive
and living my days abundantly.
I've fulfilled dreams far-reaching,
and some I once thought impossible for me,
including seeing the Taj Mahal in India,
and Machu Picchu in Peru –
true wonders of this world.
Places, monuments, seas apart, east and west.
Sunsets and sunrises,
days and nights that never seemed to end.
When my final days approach,
if you think of me at all
know that I was profusely blessed.
Above all else, let me say to you,
I discovered what really mattered
was not what I thought it to be at all.
What really counted
was the love I felt from those around me.
They sustained me throughout my journey,
and all the days of my life.
I hope I've given that love back…

My Wish for You

My wish for you

is that your reason for being

in this world is revealed.

You accept and embrace

what it is you are about.

You set a path

that enables you to fulfill your dreams,

that gives your life purpose.

A body and mind

that does not abandon you

your whole life through.

The embers are stoked,

igniting the flame that starts the fire.

The one from within

that can only be extinguished

by the one who put it there.

Blessings

This life we've been given is

perhaps random for some,

while for others clearly intentional.

It makes no difference how we are here,

just that we are here.

Let us hear of another,

his message although long ago spoken

remains forever true

from the beginning to the end of our years:

"I once was as you are. I am as you will become."

Perhaps there will come a time when you'll discover

that what you thought was important wasn't at all.

Someday, I hope soon, you'll be the one to say:

"This life I've been given I've done more than not.

At times I may have been distracted,

but I'm not looking back, only forward."

Take Not This Life for Granted

Let me not go forth and take one more breath for granted.

The years I've lived have gone by quickly.

Sometimes when looking back it all seems blurred,

to run together, indistinguishable from one year to another.

The pace I've lived I need not continue.

It is within me to determine

the significance of each and every day.

It need not be a mystery.

Too soon we surrender and yield our lives

to that which we know is inevitable.

It was to be our fate from the beginning.

An ending.

I embrace this knowledge.

It's given me more, not less,

of living in this world.

Be the Light

I wanted to make a difference with my life.

Yet, I knew I couldn't have much of an impact

if I continued sitting, holding my hands,

as if in contemplation.

So I stood up.

It was then that I realized

I could see so much more than I had imagined.

The pathway and the message became clear to me.

Be the beacon,

be the light.

It is in our light others might see.

It is in that light we all can see.

Window display in
London, England

John P. Creveling

Sometimes I Wonder

The Metro in Paris, France

Sometimes I awake in the middle of the night

and wonder:

with the time I've lived

did I get it right,

did I use my gifts and talents fully?

I like to believe I did not squander

this precious life I've been given.

It was always my intent to pass on to others

skills worthy of sharing.

They were never mine for keeping.

As with all things in life the answers aren't always clear.

There are times I feel like I'm driving a race car,

glancing in the rear-view mirror hoping to get a glimpse

of what I saw and possibly the things I missed

all while moving forward at 100 mph,

looking for the next adventure.

Sometimes I wish it were as easy

as hearing the bellowing of thunder.

After the storm when the dark clouds are gone,

the sky is clear, the radiant sun suddenly appears,

and in that instant you know,

you know what is dear.

Perhaps if I were able to predict the future,

I'd live without fear.

I'd go for it all while I was here.

Maybe then I'd know I got it right.

I'm not sure when we know.

But for me,

I'll continue on the path I'm on,

believing this one's for me.

And in my journey if I should discover a four-leaf clover,

I'll pick it up and wish that good fortune

shines upon you and me for all of eternity.

We Are Here — We Have Arrived

It's amazing how quickly the present becomes the past
and we start looking back at our once-hurried pace,
never really mindful of how long it would last.
As I think about it now there were times
when it seemed like a race.
Yet, there was no competition.
We were not running to a predetermined finish line.
We don't get to retrace our steps.
We move through time as if it were endless,
with all-too-little thought about its inevitable ending.
Here we are at this place we once thought to be so far off.
Almost unexpectedly we are here now,
whether we want to be or not.
We don't have refusal rights.
We don't get to postpone our arrival.
We may wish some moments could be repeated—
savoring what we loved and getting right
what we wish we could do over.
But we're not in a movie,
there are no moments of a "second take."
Too soon our strides give way to an uncharacteristic gait
and shuffling of feet.
Although we may not be ready
to enter this phase in our lives,
there is no retreating.

There'll be no negotiations.

In spite of our protestations we are here.

This is our new journey.

Welcome!

LIVE, LIVE, LIVE!

Make no mistake as you read this verse.

It is life I celebrate!

Although it may seem a bit perverse

as I traverse

between the now and what will be.

I'd like to concede

the truth that we know

we need not debate

nor can we avoid

our inevitable fate.

A time will arrive for us all

when our vision will fade,

we'll speak no more,

a last breath will emerge,

and our once-vivid memories

will ultimately recede,

and we'll be no more.

I wish it would occur to us sooner,

that we realize the brevity of our lives,

and not squander nor waste our time

on things that really don't matter.

We get no second chance,

there'll be no dispensation.

Now is our time to dance.

Let us advance

and discover the resonance within,

that we know why it is we are here,

our purpose,

the reason for being in the world.

Proclaim our voice and go forth,

while it is we are able.

Chichen Itza, Mexico

John P. Creveling

This Moment

How is it possible that I am here?

I'm looking back at the life I've lived,

and maybe a little of the life I wish I lived.

I'm the fortunate one I know,

I'm here.

I may have had some tumbles,

and carry with me a few visible scars,

As well as some within, below the surface.

I have had wonderful experiences

and I'm thankful for an abundance of living.

There were many who started just like me.

Those who dreamed of a world of possibilities

who wanted so much more than what they were given.

Their voices now silent,

there'll be no reprieve.

They barely had time to be alive.

I don't know why them and not me.

In this moment of awareness,

I wish not to forget,

I've lived,

I'm able to look back

AND FORWARD!

Do You Think of Me?

Do you think of me as I think of you
and ever wonder where I am?
Do you ever look up at the stars at night
and remember how we held each other tight
well into the morning light?
Do you wish for me
what I wish for you—
health and happiness
your whole life through,
a lasting love that holds forever true?
I hope for you
more sunshine than rain.
Safe travels and fond memories
that sustain you all the days of your life.

John P. Creveling

Without Fanfare

Without fanfare,

I realize I've arrived

in full view at the place in life

known intimately by millions before,

yet once seemed distant to me.

This body in which I dwell,

the consequences of living,

has gotten me here in sickness and in health

in spite of myself.

This new path,

this new journey,

I take a bit hesitantly,

cautiously, at first.

Uncharacteristically of me,

a bit slower, unsure,

even awkward at times.

Yet, inevitably I move,

sometimes above my own protestations.

Confronted by my limitations,

imagined or otherwise

I go onward,

not always forward.

Days and nights that once seemed infinite

really are after all finite.

So it is I find myself here,

in the present,

not in the past of what has been,

but here today, and each new day,

aware and fully alive.

I will boldly live here until my last breath.

When years from now it comes my time to depart

as others before me have,

and those who will follow,

I will do so exhausted, fully spent,

knowing full well that while present in this world

I, John P. Creveling,

FULLY LIVED!

I WAS HERE!

Chris preparing to celebrate our journey to Alaska

Epilogue

First and foremost, thank you for coming along on this particular journey! Whether you looked at the photographs, artwork, or read some of the reflections or poetry expressed in this book, thank you! I hope I have provided you with something that has inspired you—perhaps a few "nuggets" in these pages.

With any luck, maybe you laughed, even if only for a brief moment. Perhaps, too, you let yourself forget and were present to being with your own feelings. If you shed any tears, may they have been tears reminding you how special this life is because you are in it. I hope there is something in this book that resonates with you.

Imagine, if this is the only life you will have—what is it you want for yourself? What will bring you joy when your hair has turned gray, your body has begun to sag in places you never thought possible, and you start looking back and reviewing your life? What do you want to be able to say in that final moment? Your last breath?

An Epilogue, by nature is a conclusion; a Prologue, an Introduction. I'm planning to continue on this path, writing, drawing, painting, finding new adventures, and other new learning opportunities. Why not? I want to continue actively engaging in life for as long as I'm able. This, my first book, is really a part of what will become our journey. Like old friends, we'll gather one day and share stories of being alive in the world. I hope that time will be soon, and often.

In the meantime, I surround you with positive energy and my heartfelt best wishes. I hope you've begun a conversation with yourself, and a discussion with others, an exploration of what your life is, in the present, and what you hope it will be, and, what you want it to be in the future. May your journey in this world be one of your choosing.

This final thought I leave for you: Years from now when you are much older, may you be able to say, "While in this world I lived!"

It Takes a Village and an Angel to Raise a Child
is the title of this artwork of mine.

My wife, Chris, is the angel, albeit any painting of angels I've ever seen didn't have red hair. I solved this dilemma by painting her hair blonde.

161

Acknowledgements

I have been blessed to have family and friends who have encouraged and inspired me. And my good fortune has been to have the support and care of a team of medical professionals and staff at the Philadelphia VA Medical Center. My thanks to Cecilia Sciamanna and the Gold Team. To Tai Chi Instructor, Marcus Julian Carbo, who volunteers his time and expertise.

As a person with Parkinson's disease (PD), I have had superlative care from Pennsylvania VA PADRECC Doctors John Duda, Jayne Wilkinson, James Morley, Michelle Fullard, and Sneha Mantri. And health-care professionals Gretchen Glenn, Eileen Hummel, Dawn McHale, Heidi Watson, Julia Wood, Joellyn Fox, Heather Cianci, Suzanne Reichwein, and others I may have accidentally overlooked.

And a special thanks to Dr. Gordon H. Baltuch who gave me a second life! To Dr. Howard Hurtig who reminded me to keep asking!

My thanks also to my longtime friend Walt Bateman, for encouragement and help. And to Sheila Haren, a hero of mine, who shows me what the word "courage" means.

Thanks, too, to the thousands of caregivers everywhere who sustain friends and family. And the PD support groups across the country, and throughout the world, who provide solace and an array of services. Thanks to Doug and Luke Cooper for their help with the book. Special thanks to Morgan Ruelle for his friendship and rescuing me when I needed technical support and expertise.

I also thank Judy Flander for help with this book, her friendship and for her gracious gift of lovingly nudging me along every step of the way!

Make time in your life for fun.

Make time to play.

Make time for living!

Philadelphia, Pa.

A Few Questions

I hope this book has been of value to you. When I finished writing it I realized that as I expressed how I feel about life, family, loved ones, faith, death, etc., there might be individuals who would like to consider a few questions about what they have read. Following are some questions to get you going. There may also be a photograph, drawing, or painting to consider as well.

- If you had an opportunity to sit and chat with me, what would you like to talk about? Why? What would you like me to write, draw, or photograph more of? Why?

- What gives you meaning and value at this time in your life? Why?

- If you were getting together with friends, what topic would you like to talk about? Why?

- What do you want to do more of? Less of? Why?

- What would you like to draw, paint, or photograph?

- If you were to write a poem, or reflection, what would it be about and why? What words would you use?

- What poems or reflections resonated with you in this book and why?